Survival Guide

10 Prepper's Tools and Weapons Out of Common Things

All photos used in this book, including the cover photo were made available under a Attribution 2.0 Generic (CC BY 2.0) and sourced from Flickr.

Table Of Contents

Introduction 4

Chapter 1 – 10 Top Survival Tools And Weapons 5

    1. The Heater 5

    2. Emergency Light 7

    3. Debris Mask 8

    4. Condoms 9

    5. Knife 12

    6. Glasses 14

    7. Shelter Building with Garbage Bags 16

    8. Signaling Equipment 18

    9. Bandana 20

    10. Rope 21

Conclusion 23

Introduction

You never know when an emergency situation may strike. No one has seen tomorrow and it is impossible to predict it. This is the reason you need to know how to become a pro at prepping skills.

When you are learning to be an efficient and skilled prepper, one of the key things which you need to do is make sure that you can come up with your list of survival tools and weapons.

There are plenty of people who think that survival tools would be very costly and it can lead to a major setback. However, this is not so. In this book, we are going to make you familiar with the 10 different survival tools and weapons which you can make out of some everyday regular things.

The idea is to ensure that with this knowledge, you should be able to make the most out of your available tool. These days, it is important to be a prepper and you have to be skilled in this art. The reason is the fact that the absence of such skills can prevent you from being your own savior.

You do not know what kind of situations may arise and so you have to ensure that you are prepared for the worst. When you know how to turn regular things into survival tools, even the worst of all situations is not going to scare you because you would know exactly how to dodge it in an apt manner.

So, are you all set to sharpen your skills and to find out some of the best ways by which you can become a pro prepper and extreme survivalist? Read this book to master the tricks of this trade and get better at it.

Chapter 1 – 10 Top Survival Tools And Weapons

Let us now take a look at 10 of the best tools and weapons which you can make yourself that is sure to serve your need. Of course, you have to be sure that you are putting in the right effort in procuring the materials and then working on it in an apt manner.

Some of them are really simple and it may serve a basic need, but when you are in an emergency situation, even the tiniest of help can turn out to be a life-changer. This is why we have made it a point to bring to you the best of both the worlds.

We are not going to emphasize a great deal upon complex DIYs where you have to put in a lot of effort simply for making the weapons because to be very honest, most of us don't even get the time for making all the powerful stuff when we are stuck.

1. The Heater

Situation: suppose you are stuck in a car and it is snowing and there is absolutely no source of heat. Sounds like a terrible place to be?

We all know how easily a person could die if there is no heating source in such cold winter condition. So, what exactly is the right solution for you? You need to find the right way by which you could get some heat. Sometimes generating even the slightest amount of heat can turn out to be a complete savior for you.

You would be surprised at the quick solution which we will offer that can be really effective. Here, we are going to help you make your own survival tool – which is the instant handmade candle. Let us see exactly how this is to be done.

Things you would need

- Tampon

- Paper clip

- Lip balm tube

Steps to follow

1. Take the tampon and remove the cotton string from it. It is important that you are very careful when you are pulling out the cotton string and you need to be really cautious and careful.

2. You can make use of a paper clip to extract the cotton string from it. Place it meticulously and draw out the string.

3. Now, take this cotton string and stick it on the tube of lip balm which you have. The lip balm contains wax and this cotton string will act like your handmade wick which will be easier to put on fire.

4. Light it at this end and you will find that a candle will glow.

Note

You should make it a point to ensure that the plastic tube should not catch fire. You can ensure this by twisting the lip balm as the wick keeps on burning. This will prevent the flame from catching fire on the tube.

This is an excellent hack which will generate a little heat and even light up the car. Not just your car, even if you are stuck in a snowy weather, you can make full use of this survival strategy as the burning candle will glow the place and even give you the much-needed heat as well.

2. Emergency Light

We all know how important it is to have a source of light. However, more often than not, it so happens that we tend to forget to carry an emergency light with us.

Situation: Suppose you were out trekking in the open or in the wild, in such cases, it is very easy to get lost. Even if you are on an expedition and you end up experiencing power outage all alone, the element of fear may be too high. In such cases, you will need a source of light to help you out.

Of course, there are plenty of ways which you can use but when you are badly stuck, you will definitely be on the lookout for an easy fix. Let us see what we have got for you.

Things you would need

- A can of oil packed tuna
- Newspaper
- Matchstick

Steps to follow

1. Make a small hole on the top of a tuna can pack with oil.
2. Now, roll a part of a newspaper (two by five inches) and push it into the wick.

3. Make sure to push the wick in the hole and when you are doing so, you need to ensure that you can leave an inch exposed.

4. Wait for some time so that the wick will thoroughly absorb the oil.

5. When the absorption is done, make sure to light it with a match.

Note

This oil lamp will burn for as long as two hours. Not only this, the good thing is that even after you have used the tuna can, it will still be good to use for your eating purpose later on.

3. Debris Mask

This will be an unconventional survivalist tool and something which you must have least likely imagined it. However, like we say drastic times call for drastic measures. This is often the situation wherein you will need to scour every possible thing you can use and this is why it comes in handy to know about this hack.

Situation: In case you find yourself amidst a fire breakout or even in situations when the air around you is extremely smoky and it is getting very hard you breathe, this hack will surely help you survive.

It is important to note that it is crucial to make sure that the air you breathe is pure and devoid of too many germs. Polluted air can be a cause of a lot of problems and this will surely turn out to be the cause of a lot more hassles.

Things you would need

- A bra cup

Steps to follow

1. Take off your bra and make sure to dust it once before using.

2. Ideally, for best use, it should be sweat-free and should be clean for your use.

3. You can use the cups to cover your nose and even your mouth area. We do know that it isn't the healthiest option, but when you are in an emergency situation and the air around you is dangerous, using a bra cup can be a good choice.

4. If you need your hands for carrying out other activities, make sure to tie the bra straps around your head region. This will fix the cup in place and you can concentrate on other work while keeping your hands absolutely free.

Note

This isn't a long term solution and when you are using this hack, you need to be sure that you should try and look for a safe solution as soon as possible. Of course, it doesn't look nice if you move around in your bra cup for a long time, but when an emergency strikes, you will need to do with whatever immediate solutions you may have.

4. Condoms

As strange as it may sound, a condom serves a wide variety of uses. If you thought that a condom was only used for the sake of practicing safe sex, you are so wrong.

There are multiple uses of a condom and when you are familiar with it, it is sure to help you. Sometimes even in extreme situations, it is your condoms, which will turn out to be useful.

If you think it is a tacky move, you need to know that when you are battling for survival, you need to makeshift with whatever you have. So, even if you are headed for a trek, stacking a few condoms with you might be an excellent idea.

Things you would need

- A condom

Steps to follow

Using a condom in a survival solution isn't rocket science. You might still be wondering as to what use it is really going to serve. Well, let us explain it to you.

A condom is highly stretchable – we all know it. So, you can fill it with water, which can turn out to be extremely useful in situations when you feel like you may dehydrate or die out of thirst. As per reports, a tiny condom could hold up to a gallon of water, which is quite enough to help you survive for one whole day.

The trick here is how to fill a condom, right?

If you can find a flowing source of water somewhere like say a tap or maybe even a nozzle, you could simply put the condom underneath it and the high pressure of water will fill it and make it full. You can then stack the tiny condom and carry it with you. Every time you are thirsty, take in a sip and head ahead.

However, the real trouble arises when you are stuck in situations where there is no kitchen tap or nozzle. You may come across a pond or a lake. Wondering how to fill the condom in such cases?

The trick is simple again. All you need to do is stretch out the bottom neck of the condom. When you do this, it will help you fill the condom with relative ease. One other use of a condom when you are looking for a survival tool is for stacking lifesaving items.

Think of a situation wherein there is a lot of water, say you are stuck in a flash flood. Of course, you need to make sure that some of your vital elements are dry and they do not get submerged. We are not talking of huge items like batteries or your cell phones but think of tiny stuff like a matchstick.

If all your matchsticks get wet, will you be able to light a fire which can help you in getting some light? Of course not! This is why you need to find a way to keep them dry. Yes, you guessed it right. Once again, you can fall on your condoms.

Simply add your small necessary items in the condom and they will stay intact as water won't reach inside it and this is sure to help you out.

You might be quite shocked as to how condoms can be used in times when you need to be a survivalist. However, it is important to know these facts as it will help you become an excellent prepper who can make the most of all kinds of situations.

5. Knife

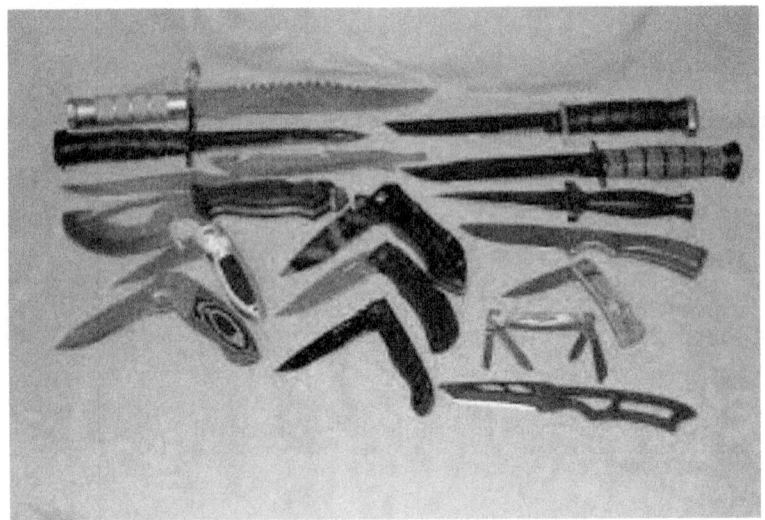

Source: here

When we are talking of survival tools, of course, you need a knife. There are plenty of purposes which a knife can serve and you should make it a point to ensure that you know how to put a knife to right use.

Let us first make you familiar with the varied uses which a knife has to offer.

• Knives can help you in cutting the ropes which can help you if you are stuck in trekking situations.

• It can also act as a weapon which will aid in keeping the wild animals at bay. You never know what you may run into and this is why having a knife would help in keeping the wild animals away.

- Even when you are in need of starting a fire, it is a knife which will come in handy. You can use a bow drill for the sake of starting a fire and it is surely going to help you in both lighting a place and even for your own safety purposes as well.

- You can also use the knives for the sake of building different kinds of emergency shelters as well. This will help you cut the branches and even aid in making a perfect tent too.

These are some of the varied ways by which you can use a knife in extreme situations where you are in need of the survival tools and weapons. You can sharpen a knife and even put it to multiple uses. Of course, you need to make sure that you are maintaining the knife in an apt manner too, such that the edges are sharp and it can help you to easily perform the different activities.

Here are some of the important tips which you need to keep in mind when you are looking to handle your knife in an apt manner.

- Make it a point not to use a folding knife. Folding knives tend to get loosened after using for a certain period of time. Make it a point to turn the screw as it comes with a screw attached below the knife. Tighten the screw from time to time, but use a smaller knife rather than opting for a folded one.

- Also, you should make it a point to sharpen your knife at regular intervals. When you are having a knife which isn't sharp, it won't serve the need as it might not be able to help you cut the ropes and even tree barks as well.

- Also, make sure not to leave a knife wet when you are stacking it away. Wet knives tend to rust very quickly and this is surely going to create a lot of troubles. Always, use a damp cloth to wipe off your knife and then keep it in your bag.

So, you can opt for knives and this is sure to help you in stacking it in the right manner. When you want to hone your survival skills, there is no way you can do without a knife.

6. Glasses

This might seem strange, but glasses can help you drastically in an unforeseen situation. If you wear vision glasses and are trapped in a situation where you are supposed to build a fire or create some distressing signals, then glasses can be of great help to you. Consider yourself lucky if you own a pair of vision glasses as they can help you save your life.

Situation: Suppose you are trapped somewhere and you need to build a fire. In such an unfavorable case, if you own vision glasses, you can ignite some fire without using a lighter or a matchstick. All you need is some paper and your pair of glasses. Also, they can be used to signal others about your location. Let's figure out how we can achieve the same.

How to use glasses to create a signal?

1. If you are trapped somewhere and would like to flash some signal about your location, then use your vision glasses to achieve it. Start by taking them out of your pocket or your eyes.

2. Now, try reflecting the sun's rays with your glasses in order to create distress signals. Try flashing it on solid and dark surfaces nearby and keep on moving them.

3. If a rescue person is passing or is nearby, then they can easily locate you by guessing the source of the signal.

Not just the glass, if you want to create a tool, then you can simply dismantle them and use the wire of the frame to create a hook of some kind.

How to use glasses to start a fire?

You must have tried doing this when you were a kid. It is just like using a mirror to ignite a paper or a volatile substance on fire. If your lens is made up of glass, instead of those plastic materials, and you have a convex lens, you can easily use it to start a fire. A convex lens is used by people who are suffering from a flaw in their farsightedness.

1. Start by collecting objects that are lightweight and can easily catch fire. You can either use a dry cloth like your socks, some leaves, or even a piece of paper.

2. Now, you need to keep your lens at a distance of around 30 centimeters away from the object that you need to set on fire.

3. Place your glass between the sun's rays and the object so that it will form a small spot on the object.

4. The object will start smoldering after a few minutes. You can now simply blow it gently and put other supporting objects to make sure that the fire is now stable.

Note

After when you have set the fire, try to be awake. You don't want the fire to damage your surrounding area or set the entire atmosphere on fire. This will cause more damage to you than help. One should always be really careful when it comes to fire and should handle it with utmost care.

7. Shelter Building with Garbage Bags

Source: <u>here</u>

If you are going for a hiking or trekking expedition, then always carry a few garbage bags with you. Not only, will they help you keep the environment clear by collecting your mess and letting the natural space pollution free, but if used wisely, they can help you save your life.

Situation: Consider that you are out in the wild and have lost your way home. In the open area, you need to survive without any water, food, or shelter. Alone and with no point of contact with the outer world, you need to have a few tools by your side to help you survive the night. Garbage bags are those everyday objects that every prepper should have stuffed in their backpacks as they can be used to serve various purposes.

How to create a shelter using garbage bags?

If you are trapped somewhere and you need to survive by creating a safe place for yourself, then a few garbage bags can help you build your shelter.

Use some rope, a few tree branches or a trap to tie your garbage bags together. This won't even take a lot of time and you don't have to use leaves or other natural things to cover you. A natural shelter created by leaves can get damp after rain, but not this one. Since garbage bags are made of plastic, not only will they keep you safe from water, but also from the heat of the sun.

Other uses of garbage bags

If you have a few garbage bags with you when you are out and lost, you can always use them to cover your backpack. You can simply place all your essentials inside the backpack and in order to make sure that it stays protected, simply place a garbage bag over it. Cover it tightly to make sure that no water or air can harm it. This will be of great help to you during a storm or heavy rainfall.

You can also use a huge garbage bag to create a rain jacket out of it. Simply cut a hole in the top of it and put your head through it. Try to wrap it around your body as tightly as possible. This will make it function like a rain jacket, by keeping you warm and dry.

If you are out in the wild, and would like to sleep, then fill the garbage bag with some leaves or soft materials that are accessible nearby. This will make you create a natural pillow or mattress of your own, so that you won't have to sleep on the ground.

When you are heading out to a lake or a water body nearby, you can always fill fresh water in an empty bag. If you want to collect rainfall, then use a garbage bag to collect the precipitation and use it as per your convenience. Simply dig a hole and cover it with the bag to collect water.

8. Signaling Equipment

Source: here

When you are lost and are away from your friends or family, you need some sorts of signaling equipment to let them know about your whereabouts. An essential tool for every prepper, signaling equipment like a whistle or a signal mirror can help you substantially in order to let others find you.

Situation: Any signaling equipment can be used in various situations. Suppose that you are out camping and is lost from your gang. You would need a way to contact with your friends in order to let them know about your location. In the case of any natural disaster like an earthquake, when you are amidst of piles of trash, you need to let a rescue person know about your location. In such an adverse scenario, if you have something to signal, then it can help you save your life.

Often, cell phones and other new-age communication methods don't work in the wild or when you are hit with a disaster. In such an unforeseen situation, you can use a signal mirror or a flashlight to let others know of your location. A proper flash can be seen by people who are miles away from you or are flying in an aircraft.

Signal Mirror

In case, if you are trapped in an isolated place and you see an aircraft nearby, you can flash signals across the sky. Try to use different patterns while signaling or simply flash for S.O.S. to let the pilot know that it is being made by a human being who is in danger.

Try to engrave proper instructions just behind your signal mirror so that you never forget how to use it. Also, if you are lending it to someone else, they can simply get to know about its correct usage with a single look.

Take proper care of your signal mirror by placing it in a pouch to avoid the occurrence of any scratches.

Whistles

Just like a signal mirror, other signaling equipment which is of great use is whistles. No one can avoid the sound of a man-made whistle when they are in trouble. No matter how lost you are; you can always use either artificial whistle or a man-made sound to signal people nearby.

There might be instances when you don't have an artificial whistle with you. In such cases, you can always blow a whistle using your mouth and hands. One should always know how to whistle in order to make sure that they are able to signal others properly.

Not just letting others know of your location, a whistle can be used to alarm them of a nearby danger or let them know that you are injured.

Smoke

Smoke is another thing that can be used to signal others of your whereabouts. If you are lost and you know people are coming to look for you, then use a matchstick or a lighter and collect a few dry leaves from nearby to build smoke. This will let others know of your exact location.

Flashlight

A flashlight is again one of the best ways to give signals. Not just it can let you see properly in the dark, but it can help you communicate to others by using Morse code.

9. Bandana

Lightweight, cheap, and extremely easy to use, a bandana is a must-have accessory that every prepper out there should have. It comes in handy and can be placed easily in your bag, no matter when or where you are heading out. This simple accessory is not only stylish and good looking, but it can be used in plenty of scenarios.

If you are lost in the woods, you can always wear your neon colored bandana in order to be easily found. If you are wearing such a fluorescent color, people might notice your presence from a distance.

Obviously, a bandana can help you protect your head from sun or rain. A bandana is one such accessory that is helpful in both hot as well as cold situations. When you are facing the sun, simply cover your forehead with a bandana to keep it protected. Likewise, in the cold, a bandana can help you keep your head warm.

If you are being surrounded in a dusty situation where you are not able to breathe properly, then a bandana can come to your aid. You can simply cover your nostrils with it and inhale sufficient air through it. It will filter the air, keeping the pollutants and large dust particles away.

In case if you are injured or wounded, then you can use a bandana as a bandage. It will stop you from bleeding and getting your wound exposed. Not just to stop bleeding, a clean bandana can help you keep your bleed disinfected as well.

With such a wide usage, a bandana is one such accessory that should be present in every prepper's backpack. A bandana comes handy and won't cost you much at all. Though, it certainly comes with a diverse usage.

10. Rope

A Rope is probably the most useful tool that every individual should have with them. Helping you survive a worst-case scenario, a rope can be used for multiple purposes. Not just a simple rope, you should also prefer wearing a paracord bracelet. It is extremely stylish and can be used by untangling it. From a parachute cord to a jute rope, try having at least one or the other thing in your backpack whenever you are heading out.

Paracord Bracelet

A special mention of paracord bracelet should be made, as it is one object that is often forgotten by almost everyone. A paracord bracelet can be used to tighten it with something else.

One of the best characteristics about it is that it expands a little when it becomes wet and tightens up after getting dry. You can simply secure an object like a knife or a walking stick with a paracord bracelet and make it wet. It will secure a tight grip on the object after it becomes dry.

Objects like a rope, parachute cord or a paracord bracelet have some amazing and helpful functions. Some of them are as follows:

- Helping you build an emergency shelter
- A rope can assist you climb a mountain
- It can help you host your food above so that you can keep it safe from the animals
- A splint can be created for any broken bones with a rope
- It can assist you to make traps for fishes and animals while hunting
- Attaching gears and other essentials with your pack, and more

There are literally countless of instances when a rope can help you save your life. Every prepper should keep a rope in their car and one in their backpack, every time they are heading out. It doesn't mean if you are trapped inside or if you are out there in the wild, but a rope can help you change any situation drastically. Extremely cheap and lightweight, ropes should be placed in every individual's backpack as an essential.

Conclusion

Congratulations on finishing the guide in such a short time! We are sure that you must have enjoyed reading it. A prepper should always be ready to face the worst of scenarios as bad times always come unannounced. With these essential set of tools and weapons, your chances of survival surely increase drastically. It doesn't matter if you are trapped somewhere inside or if you are out there in the wild, all alone and lost, but these everyday tools can help you prepare yourself without much hassle.

Constructed from everyday objects and other household things, these tools won't cost you a dime. From garbage bags to ropes, and from bandanas to glasses, several everyday objects have been mentioned in the guide with their diverse usage.

Who knew that something so ordinary could be of such great usage in an emergency situation? The next time when a disaster hit or an unforeseen situation comes, you know that you are ready with all the essential goods.

Try creating an emergency kit of a backpack and stuff it with these essential tools and weapons so that you can have everything important at one place. Though, there are a lot of other things like a compass or a lighter that must be included in your emergency kit. But these are basic objects that every prepper already has in their emergency kits.

With this guide, we tried to explore cheap and useful everyday goods that can be of great help to you. Never be sorry, when you are in the middle of a disaster. Know your way out, signal others, and give your very best shot in order to survive.

We are sure that these essential tools and weapons would be of diverse use to you, letting you save your life when any adverse situation would come.

FREE Bonus Reminder

If you have not grabbed it yet, please go ahead and download your special bonus report *"DIY Projects. 13 Useful & Easy To Make DIY Projects To Save Money & Improve Your Home!"*
Simply Click the Button Below

OR **Go to This Page**
http://preppersliving.com/free

BONUS #2: More Free Books
Do you want to receive more Free Books?
We have a mailing list where we send out our new Books when they go free on Kindle. Click on the link below to sign up for Free Book Promotions.
=> **Sign Up for Free Book Promotions** <=

OR Go to this URL
http://zbit.ly/1WBb1Ek

Printed in Great Britain
by Amazon